You have an amazing brain in your head!

Your brain has many different parts, each with a different job. These parts work together to help you learn and do different things.

- Attention and decisions
- Where things are
- What you see
- What you hear
- Balance and coordination

In the middle of your brain there are parts in charge of emotions, memory, and getting information from your senses.

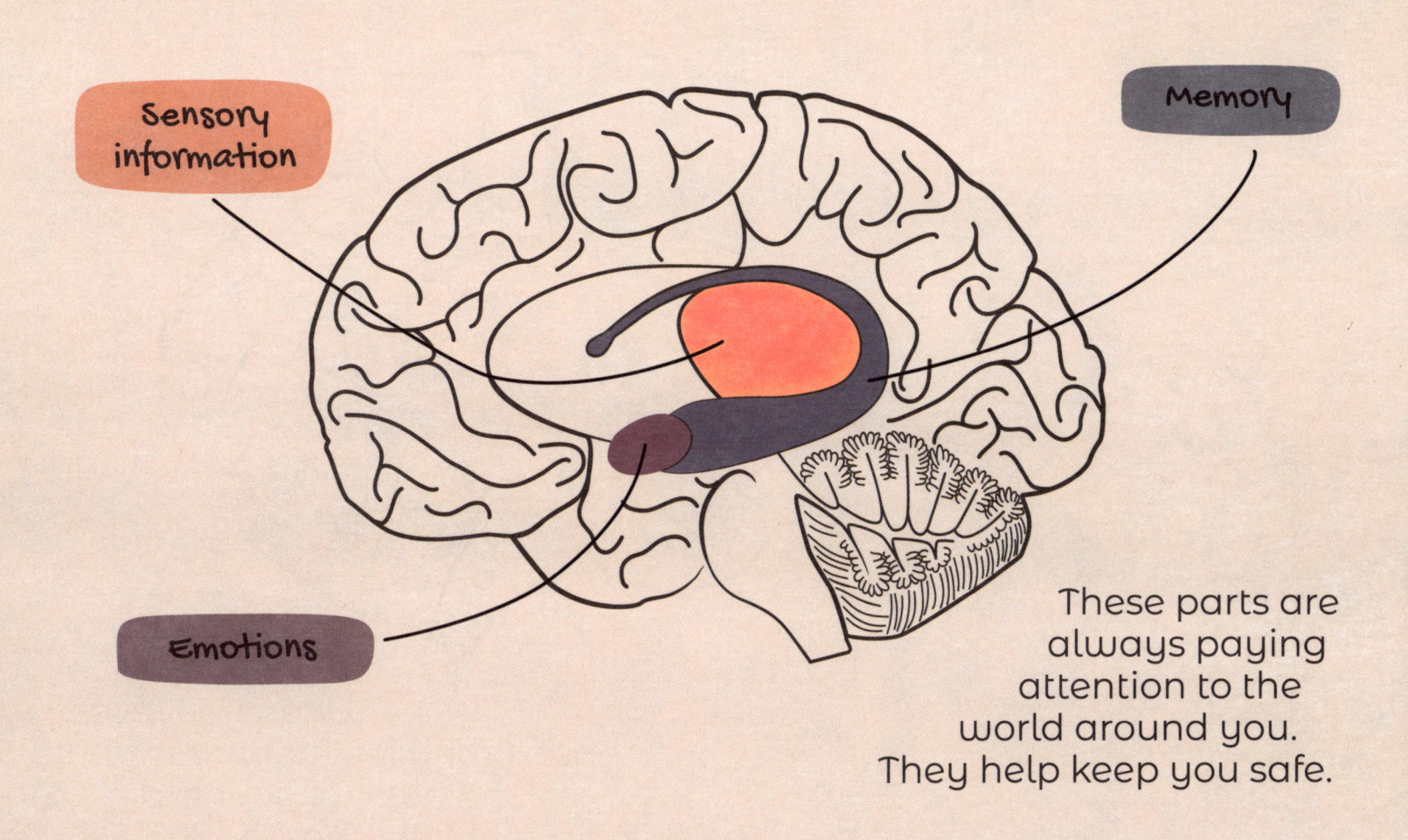

Sensory information

Memory

Emotions

These parts are always paying attention to the world around you. They help keep you safe.

Sometimes these parts get very excited by strong feelings. This can make it hard to think!

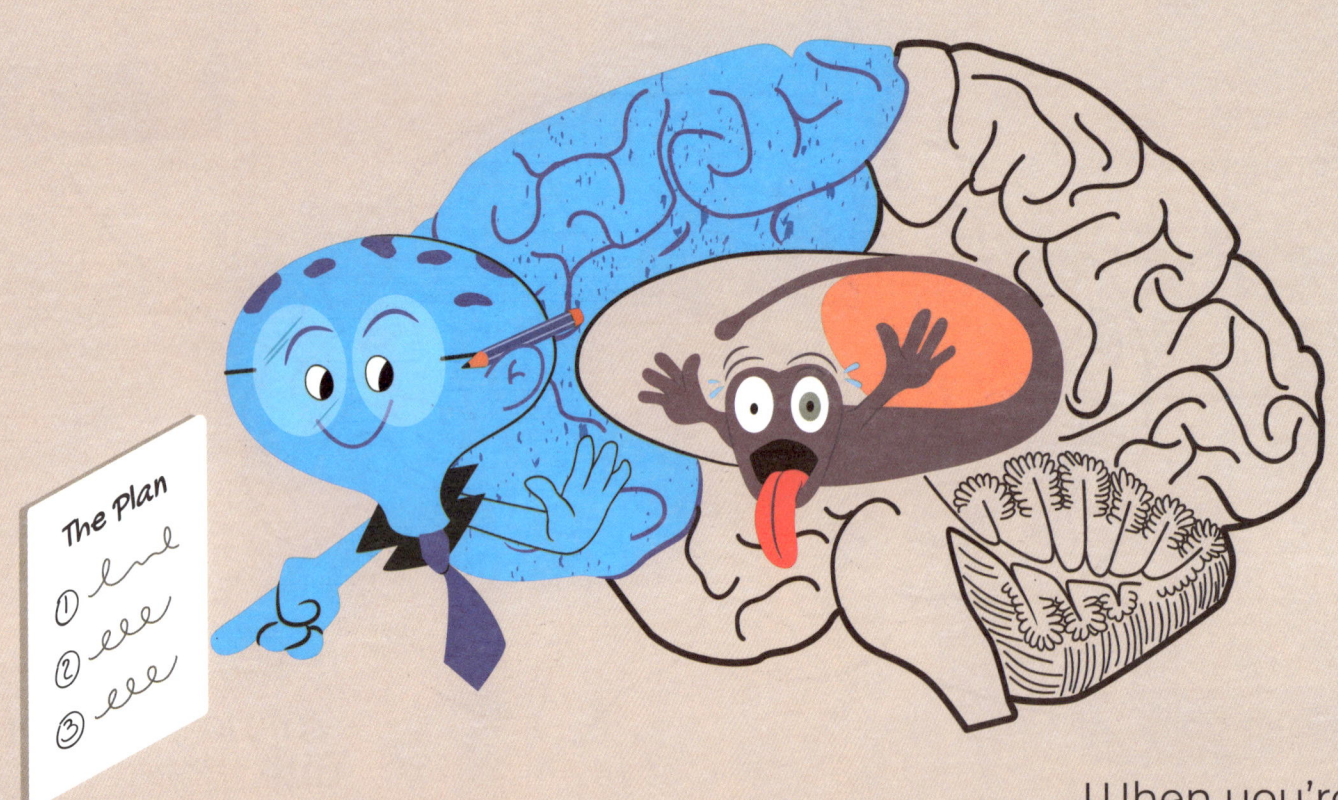

When you're feeling those strong feelings, your frontal lobe - or "the boss" of your brain - can help you figure out what to do.

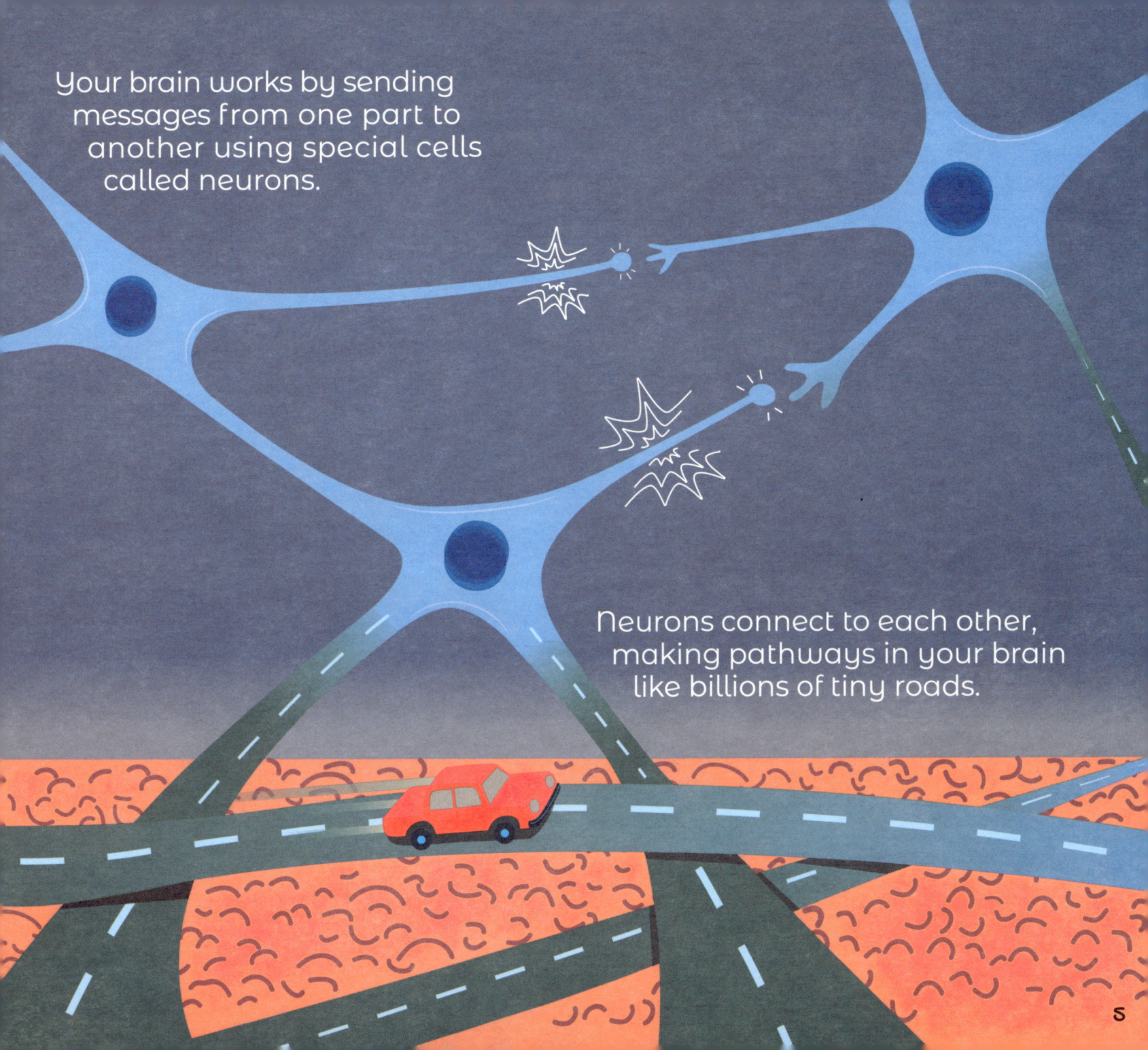

Your brain works by sending messages from one part to another using special cells called neurons.

Neurons connect to each other, making pathways in your brain like billions of tiny roads.

When you have a thought or want to do something, your brain sends messages along these roads, like cars bringing information from one place to the next.

As you think new thoughts and try new things, your brain builds new roads, even when you're an adult!

There are many things your brain makes easy for you to do. These are your brain's highways, where the messages travel at super fast speeds!

Your highways may be things that come easily to you, like...

speed limit: **SUPER FAST**

When you try something new or difficult, it may take a little longer for the messages to get where they need to go. That's because the roads are still under construction.

For example, when you were little, you may remember that at first it was hard to…

But not anymore!

Now, after a bunch of practice and hard work, the roads are built and your brain knows exactly where to go.

That's called learning!

Sometimes your brain doesn't make it easy for you to get from one place to another. When your brain is having a tough time, you may feel frustrated, embarrassed, or just plain tired!

For example, your brain may be working extra hard to…

But never fear!

Your brain is making new connections every day.

With a little help and some great tools, you can make those tricky roads much easier to travel. You might even find a totally new way to get there that no one has ever thought of before!

You should know that lots of people's brains have highways and construction zones that are very similar to yours.

So many, in fact, that there are special words to describe what's going on.

Here are some helpful words for understanding your brain:

You should also know that you have a whole crew of construction workers who are there to help you build your brain!

Who are the people helping you to create new connections and build new brain roads?

13

Finally, you've got tools!

What tools or strategies will help you build your brain?

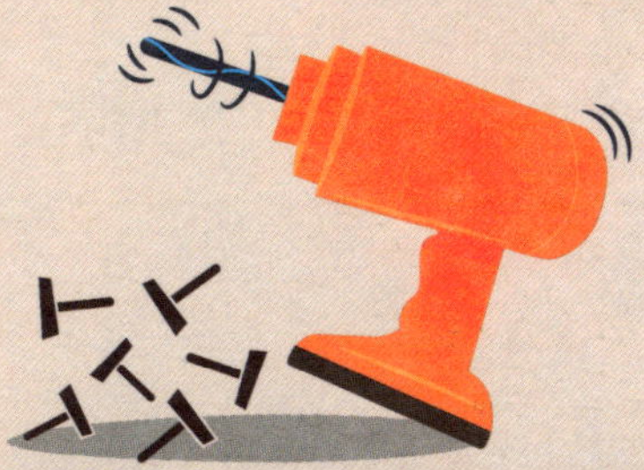

Your brain will take you to incredible places!

Congratulations on building such an amazing brain!

About the Author

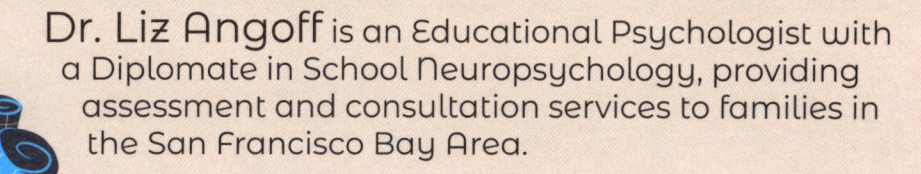

Dr. Liz Angoff is an Educational Psychologist with a Diplomate in School Neuropsychology, providing assessment and consultation services to families in the San Francisco Bay Area.

Learn more about Dr. Liz at www.DrLizAngoff.com.

About the Illustrators

Dr. Andrew Falk is a science educator who has worked as a classroom teacher, teacher educator, and curriculum designer.

Andrés González is a digital illustrator, specializing in translating ideas into drawings for educational purposes. Learn more about Andrés at www.AndresChimp.com.

Notes